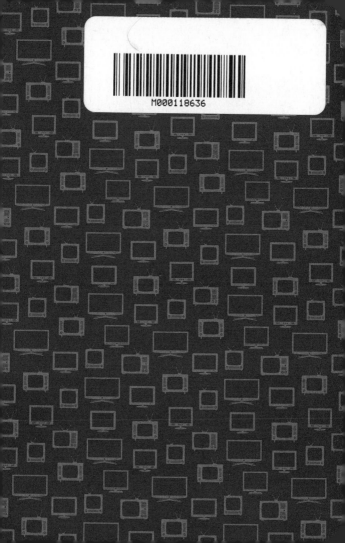

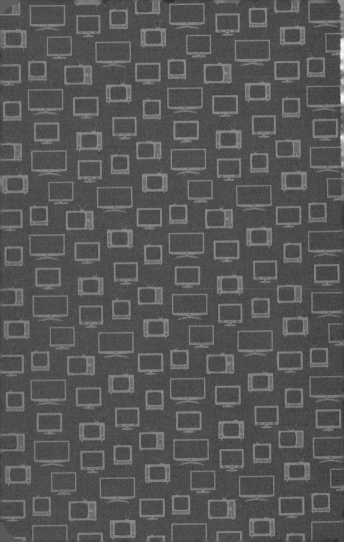

WHAT
ARE YOU
WATCHING?
LOGBOOK

Keep Track of
Your TV Shows!

PETER PAUPER PRESS, INC.
White Plains, New York

PETER PAUPER PRESS
Fine Books and Gifts Since 1928

Our Company

In 1928, at the age of twenty-two, Peter Beilenson began printing books on a small press in the basement of his parents' home in Larchmont, New York. Peter—and later, his wife, Edna—sought to create fine books that sold at "prices even a pauper could afford."

Today, still family owned and operated, Peter Pauper Press continues to honor our founders' legacy—and our customers' expectations—of beauty, quality, and value.

Images used under license from Shutterstock.com

Designed by Tesslyn Pandarakalam

Copyright © 2020
Peter Pauper Press, Inc.
202 Mamaroneck Avenue
White Plains, NY 10601 USA
ISBN 978-1-4413-3297-4
Printed in China
7 6 5 4 3 2 1

Visit us at www.peterpauper.com

INTRODUCTION

If you've ever lost track of which episode or season of a show you're watching, or tend to forget the names of shows that family, friends, or colleagues recommend, this book is for you!

- **MY SHOWS** log pages provide space to record **Show Title**, **Network/Streaming Service**, **Start Date**, **Day/Night/Time**, **Season**, **Total Seasons**, **Episode Length**, and **Total Episodes** for the shows you're currently watching.

  Track which **Episode** you're on—check off or fill in the number of each episode after you watch it, for up to 24 episodes.

  Write down the **Plot/Synopsis**, make **Notes**, record when the **New Season Begins**, and **Rate** each show.

- Go to page 132 to jot down other **SHOWS I WANT TO CHECK OUT**.

- Finally, record **STREAMING INFO**—logins, passwords, and more—in the back of this logbook for handy reference.

Never forget what season
or episode is next!

MY SHOWS

Show Title _____

Network/Streaming Service _____

Start Date _____ Day/Night/Time _____

Season # _____ Total Seasons _____

Episode Length _____ Total Episodes _____

EPISODE TRACKER

① ② ③ ④ ⑤ ⑥ ⑦ ⑧ ⑨ ⑩ ⑪ ⑫ ⑬ ⑭ ⑮ ⑯ ⑰ ⑱ ⑲ ⑳ ㉑ ㉒ ㉓ ㉔

Plot/Synopsis _____

_____

_____

Notes _____

_____

_____

_____

_____

_____

_____

_____

_____

_____

New Season Begins_____

MY RATING
★★★★★

🍿 MY SHOWS 📺

Show Title _____

Network/Streaming Service _____

Start Date _____ Day/Night/Time _____

Season # _____ Total Seasons _____

Episode Length _____ Total Episodes _____

EPISODE TRACKER

① ② ③ ④ ⑤ ⑥ ⑦ ⑧ ⑨ ⑩ ⑪ ⑫ ⑬ ⑭ ⑮ ⑯ ⑰ ⑱ ⑲ ⑳ ㉑ ㉒ ㉓ ㉔

Plot/Synopsis _____

_____

_____

Notes _____

_____

_____

_____

_____

_____

_____

_____

_____

_____

MY RATING

New Season Begins_____ ⭐⭐⭐⭐⭐

🍿 MY SHOWS 📺

Show Title _____

Network/Streaming Service _____

Start Date _____ Day/Night/Time _____

Season # _____ Total Seasons _____

Episode Length _____ Total Episodes _____

EPISODE TRACKER

① ② ③ ④ ⑤ ⑥ ⑦ ⑧ ⑨ ⑩ ⑪ ⑫ ⑬ ⑭ ⑮ ⑯ ⑰ ⑱ ⑲ ⑳ ㉑ ㉒ ㉓ ㉔

Plot/Synopsis _____

_____

_____

Notes _____

_____

_____

_____

_____

_____

_____

_____

_____

MY RATING
⭐⭐⭐⭐⭐

New Season Begins_____

MY SHOWS

Show Title _____

Network/Streaming Service _____

Start Date _____ Day/Night/Time _____

Season # _____ Total Seasons _____

Episode Length _____ Total Episodes _____

EPISODE TRACKER

① ② ③ ④ ⑤ ⑥ ⑦ ⑧ ⑨ ⑩ ⑪ ⑫ ⑬ ⑭ ⑮ ⑯ ⑰ ⑱ ⑲ ⑳ ㉑ ㉒ ㉓ ㉔

Plot/Synopsis _____

_____

_____

Notes _____

_____

_____

_____

_____

_____

_____

_____

_____

_____

MY RATING
⭐⭐⭐⭐⭐

New Season Begins_____

🍿 MY SHOWS 📺

Show Title _____

Network/Streaming Service _____

Start Date _____ Day/Night/Time _____

Season # _____ Total Seasons _____

Episode Length _____ Total Episodes _____

EPISODE TRACKER

① ② ③ ④ ⑤ ⑥ ⑦ ⑧ ⑨ ⑩ ⑪ ⑫ ⑬ ⑭ ⑮ ⑯ ⑰ ⑱ ⑲ ⑳ ㉑ ㉒ ㉓ ㉔

Plot/Synopsis _____

_____

_____

Notes _____

_____

_____

_____

_____

_____

_____

_____

_____

MY RATING
⭐⭐⭐⭐⭐

New Season Begins_____

🍿 MY SHOWS 📺

Show Title _____

Network/Streaming Service _____

Start Date _____ Day/Night/Time _____

Season # _____ Total Seasons _____

Episode Length _____ Total Episodes _____

EPISODE TRACKER

① ② ③ ④ ⑤ ⑥ ⑦ ⑧ ⑨ ⑩ ⑪ ⑫ ⑬ ⑭ ⑮ ⑯ ⑰ ⑱ ⑲ ⑳ ㉑ ㉒ ㉓ ㉔

Plot/Synopsis _____

_____

_____

Notes _____

_____

_____

_____

_____

_____

_____

_____

_____

_____

MY RATING

New Season Begins_____ ★★★★★

9

🍿 MY SHOWS 📺

Show Title _____

Network/Streaming Service _____

Start Date _____ Day/Night/Time _____

Season # _____ Total Seasons _____

Episode Length _____ Total Episodes _____

EPISODE TRACKER

① ② ③ ④ ⑤ ⑥ ⑦ ⑧ ⑨ ⑩ ⑪ ⑫ ⑬ ⑭ ⑮ ⑯ ⑰ ⑱ ⑲ ⑳ ㉑ ㉒ ㉓ ㉔

Plot/Synopsis _____

_____

_____

Notes _____

_____

_____

_____

_____

_____

_____

_____

_____

_____

MY RATING
⭐⭐⭐⭐⭐

New Season Begins_____

🍿 MY SHOWS 📺

Show Title _____

Network/Streaming Service _____

Start Date _____ Day/Night/Time _____

Season # _____ Total Seasons _____

Episode Length _____ Total Episodes _____

EPISODE TRACKER

① ② ③ ④ ⑤ ⑥ ⑦ ⑧ ⑨ ⑩ ⑪ ⑫ ⑬ ⑭ ⑮ ⑯ ⑰ ⑱ ⑲ ⑳ ㉑ ㉒ ㉓ ㉔

Plot/Synopsis _____

_____

_____

Notes _____

_____

_____

_____

_____

_____

_____

_____

_____

_____

MY RATING

New Season Begins_____ ⭐⭐⭐⭐⭐

🍿 MY SHOWS 📺

Show Title _____

Network/Streaming Service _____

Start Date _____ Day/Night/Time _____

Season # _____ Total Seasons _____

Episode Length _____ Total Episodes _____

EPISODE TRACKER

① ② ③ ④ ⑤ ⑥ ⑦ ⑧ ⑨ ⑩ ⑪ ⑫ ⑬ ⑭ ⑮ ⑯ ⑰ ⑱ ⑲ ⑳ ㉑ ㉒ ㉓ ㉔

Plot/Synopsis _____

_____

_____

Notes _____

_____

_____

_____

_____

_____

_____

_____

_____

MY RATING

⭐ ⭐ ⭐ ⭐ ⭐

New Season Begins _____

🍿 MY SHOWS 📺

Show Title _____

Network/Streaming Service _____

Start Date _____ Day/Night/Time _____

Season # _____ Total Seasons _____

Episode Length _____ Total Episodes _____

EPISODE TRACKER

① ② ③ ④ ⑤ ⑥ ⑦ ⑧ ⑨ ⑩ ⑪ ⑫ ⑬ ⑭ ⑮ ⑯ ⑰ ⑱ ⑲ ⑳ ㉑ ㉒ ㉓ ㉔

Plot/Synopsis _____

_____

_____

Notes _____

_____

_____

_____

_____

_____

_____

_____

_____

_____

MY RATING

New Season Begins _____ ★★★★★

🍿 MY SHOWS 📺

Show Title _____

Network/Streaming Service _____

Start Date _____ Day/Night/Time _____

Season # _____ Total Seasons _____

Episode Length _____ Total Episodes _____

EPISODE TRACKER

① ② ③ ④ ⑤ ⑥ ⑦ ⑧ ⑨ ⑩ ⑪ ⑫ ⑬ ⑭ ⑮ ⑯ ⑰ ⑱ ⑲ ⑳ ㉑ ㉒ ㉓ ㉔

Plot/Synopsis _____

_____

_____

Notes _____

_____

_____

_____

_____

_____

_____

_____

_____

_____

MY RATING
⭐⭐⭐⭐⭐

New Season Begins_____

MY SHOWS

Show Title _____

Network/Streaming Service _____

Start Date _____ Day/Night/Time _____

Season # _____ Total Seasons _____

Episode Length _____ Total Episodes _____

EPISODE TRACKER

① ② ③ ④ ⑤ ⑥ ⑦ ⑧ ⑨ ⑩ ⑪ ⑫ ⑬ ⑭ ⑮ ⑯ ⑰ ⑱ ⑲ ⑳ ㉑ ㉒ ㉓ ㉔

Plot/Synopsis _____

_____

_____

Notes _____

_____

_____

_____

_____

_____

_____

_____

_____

_____

_____

MY RATING

★★★★★

New Season Begins_____

🍿 MY SHOWS 📺

Show Title _____

Network/Streaming Service _____

Start Date _____ Day/Night/Time _____

Season # _____ Total Seasons _____

Episode Length _____ Total Episodes _____

EPISODE TRACKER

① ② ③ ④ ⑤ ⑥ ⑦ ⑧ ⑨ ⑩ ⑪ ⑫ ⑬ ⑭ ⑮ ⑯ ⑰ ⑱ ⑲ ⑳ ㉑ ㉒ ㉓ ㉔

Plot/Synopsis _____

_____

_____

Notes _____

_____

_____

_____

_____

_____

_____

_____

_____

_____

MY RATING

New Season Begins _____ ⭐⭐⭐⭐⭐

🍿 MY SHOWS 📺

Show Title _____

Network/Streaming Service _____

Start Date _____ Day/Night/Time _____

Season # _____ Total Seasons _____

Episode Length _____ Total Episodes _____

EPISODE TRACKER

① ② ③ ④ ⑤ ⑥ ⑦ ⑧ ⑨ ⑩ ⑪ ⑫ ⑬ ⑭ ⑮ ⑯ ⑰ ⑱ ⑲ ⑳ ㉑ ㉒ ㉓ ㉔

Plot/Synopsis _____

_____

_____

Notes _____

_____

_____

_____

_____

_____

_____

_____

_____

MY RATING

New Season Begins_____ ⭐⭐⭐⭐⭐

MY SHOWS

Show Title _____

Network/Streaming Service _____

Start Date _____ Day/Night/Time _____

Season # _____ Total Seasons _____

Episode Length _____ Total Episodes _____

EPISODE TRACKER

① ② ③ ④ ⑤ ⑥ ⑦ ⑧ ⑨ ⑩ ⑪ ⑫ ⑬ ⑭ ⑮ ⑯ ⑰ ⑱ ⑲ ⑳ ㉑ ㉒ ㉓ ㉔

Plot/Synopsis _____

_____

_____

Notes _____

_____

_____

_____

_____

_____

_____

_____

MY RATING

⭐⭐⭐⭐⭐

New Season Begins_____

🍿 MY SHOWS 📺

Show Title _____

Network/Streaming Service _____

Start Date _____ Day/Night/Time _____

Season # _____ Total Seasons _____

Episode Length _____ Total Episodes _____

EPISODE TRACKER

① ② ③ ④ ⑤ ⑥ ⑦ ⑧ ⑨ ⑩ ⑪ ⑫ ⑬ ⑭ ⑮ ⑯ ⑰ ⑱ ⑲ ⑳ ㉑ ㉒ ㉓ ㉔

Plot/Synopsis _____

_____

_____

Notes _____

_____

_____

_____

_____

_____

_____

_____

_____

_____

MY RATING

New Season Begins_____ ⭐⭐⭐⭐⭐

🍿 MY SHOWS 📺

Show Title _____

Network/Streaming Service _____

Start Date _____ Day/Night/Time _____

Season # _____ Total Seasons _____

Episode Length _____ Total Episodes _____

EPISODE TRACKER

① ② ③ ④ ⑤ ⑥ ⑦ ⑧ ⑨ ⑩ ⑪ ⑫ ⑬ ⑭ ⑮ ⑯ ⑰ ⑱ ⑲ ⑳ ㉑ ㉒ ㉓ ㉔

Plot/Synopsis _____

_____

_____

Notes _____

_____

_____

_____

_____

_____

_____

_____

MY RATING
⭐⭐⭐⭐⭐

New Season Begins_____

Show Title _____

Network/Streaming Service _____

Start Date _____ Day/Night/Time _____

Season # _____ Total Seasons _____

Episode Length _____ Total Episodes _____

EPISODE TRACKER

① ② ③ ④ ⑤ ⑥ ⑦ ⑧ ⑨ ⑩ ⑪ ⑫ ⑬ ⑭ ⑮ ⑯ ⑰ ⑱ ⑲ ⑳ ㉑ ㉒ ㉓ ㉔

Plot/Synopsis _____

_____

_____

Notes _____

_____

_____

_____

_____

_____

_____

_____

_____

MY RATING

New Season Begins_____ ★ ★ ★ ★ ★

🍿 MY SHOWS 📺

Show Title _____

Network/Streaming Service _____

Start Date _____ Day/Night/Time _____

Season # _____ Total Seasons _____

Episode Length _____ Total Episodes _____

EPISODE TRACKER

① ② ③ ④ ⑤ ⑥ ⑦ ⑧ ⑨ ⑩ ⑪ ⑫ ⑬ ⑭ ⑮ ⑯ ⑰ ⑱ ⑲ ⑳ ㉑ ㉒ ㉓ ㉔

Plot/Synopsis _____

_____

_____

Notes _____

_____

_____

_____

_____

_____

_____

_____

_____

MY RATING

⭐ ⭐ ⭐ ⭐ ⭐

New Season Begins _____

🍿 MY SHOWS 📺

Show Title _____

Network/Streaming Service _____

Start Date _____ Day/Night/Time _____

Season # _____ Total Seasons _____

Episode Length _____ Total Episodes _____

EPISODE TRACKER

① ② ③ ④ ⑤ ⑥ ⑦ ⑧ ⑨ ⑩ ⑪ ⑫ ⑬ ⑭ ⑮ ⑯ ⑰ ⑱ ⑲ ⑳ ㉑ ㉒ ㉓ ㉔

Plot/Synopsis _____

_____

_____

Notes _____

_____

_____

_____

_____

_____

_____

_____

_____

_____

MY RATING

New Season Begins_____ ⭐⭐⭐⭐⭐

Show Title _____

Network/Streaming Service _____

Start Date _____ Day/Night/Time _____

Season # _____ Total Seasons _____

Episode Length _____ Total Episodes _____

EPISODE TRACKER

① ② ③ ④ ⑤ ⑥ ⑦ ⑧ ⑨ ⑩ ⑪ ⑫ ⑬ ⑭ ⑮ ⑯ ⑰ ⑱ ⑲ ⑳ ㉑ ㉒ ㉓ ㉔

Plot/Synopsis _____

_____

_____

Notes _____

_____

_____

_____

_____

_____

_____

_____

_____

MY RATING

New Season Begins_____ ⭐⭐⭐⭐⭐

🍿 MY SHOWS 📺

Show Title _____

Network/Streaming Service _____

Start Date _____ Day/Night/Time _____

Season # _____ Total Seasons _____

Episode Length _____ Total Episodes _____

EPISODE TRACKER

① ② ③ ④ ⑤ ⑥ ⑦ ⑧ ⑨ ⑩ ⑪ ⑫ ⑬ ⑭ ⑮ ⑯ ⑰ ⑱ ⑲ ⑳ ㉑ ㉒ ㉓ ㉔

Plot/Synopsis _____

_____

_____

Notes _____

_____

_____

_____

_____

_____

_____

_____

_____

_____

MY RATING

New Season Begins_____ ⭐⭐⭐⭐⭐

🍿 MY SHOWS 📺

Show Title _____

Network/Streaming Service _____

Start Date _____ Day/Night/Time _____

Season # _____ Total Seasons _____

Episode Length _____ Total Episodes _____

EPISODE TRACKER

① ② ③ ④ ⑤ ⑥ ⑦ ⑧ ⑨ ⑩ ⑪ ⑫ ⑬ ⑭ ⑮ ⑯ ⑰ ⑱ ⑲ ⑳ ㉑ ㉒ ㉓ ㉔

Plot/Synopsis _____

_____

_____

Notes _____

_____

_____

_____

_____

_____

_____

_____

MY RATING

New Season Begins_____ ⭐⭐⭐⭐⭐

🍿 MY SHOWS 📺

Show Title _____

Network/Streaming Service _____

Start Date _____ Day/Night/Time _____

Season # _____ Total Seasons _____

Episode Length _____ Total Episodes _____

EPISODE TRACKER

① ② ③ ④ ⑤ ⑥ ⑦ ⑧ ⑨ ⑩ ⑪ ⑫ ⑬ ⑭ ⑮ ⑯ ⑰ ⑱ ⑲ ⑳ ㉑ ㉒ ㉓ ㉔

Plot/Synopsis _____

_____

_____

Notes _____

_____

_____

_____

_____

_____

_____

_____

_____

MY RATING

New Season Begins _____ ⭐⭐⭐⭐⭐

🍿 MY SHOWS 📺

Show Title _____

Network/Streaming Service _____

Start Date _____ Day/Night/Time _____

Season # _____ Total Seasons _____

Episode Length _____ Total Episodes _____

EPISODE TRACKER

① ② ③ ④ ⑤ ⑥ ⑦ ⑧ ⑨ ⑩ ⑪ ⑫ ⑬ ⑭ ⑮ ⑯ ⑰ ⑱ ⑲ ⑳ ㉑ ㉒ ㉓ ㉔

Plot/Synopsis _____

_____

_____

Notes _____

_____

_____

_____

_____

_____

_____

_____

_____

_____

MY RATING
⭐ ⭐ ⭐ ⭐ ⭐

New Season Begins_____

🍿 MY SHOWS 📺

Show Title _____

Network/Streaming Service _____

Start Date _____ Day/Night/Time _____

Season # _____ Total Seasons _____

Episode Length _____ Total Episodes _____

EPISODE TRACKER

① ② ③ ④ ⑤ ⑥ ⑦ ⑧ ⑨ ⑩ ⑪ ⑫ ⑬ ⑭ ⑮ ⑯ ⑰ ⑱ ⑲ ⑳ ㉑ ㉒ ㉓ ㉔

Plot/Synopsis _____

_____

_____

Notes _____

_____

_____

_____

_____

_____

_____

_____

_____

New Season Begins_____

MY RATING
⭐⭐⭐⭐⭐

🍿 MY SHOWS 📺

Show Title _____

Network/Streaming Service _____

Start Date _____ Day/Night/Time _____

Season # _____ Total Seasons _____

Episode Length _____ Total Episodes _____

EPISODE TRACKER

① ② ③ ④ ⑤ ⑥ ⑦ ⑧ ⑨ ⑩ ⑪ ⑫ ⑬ ⑭ ⑮ ⑯ ⑰ ⑱ ⑲ ⑳ ㉑ ㉒ ㉓ ㉔

Plot/Synopsis _____

_____

_____

Notes _____

_____

_____

_____

_____

_____

_____

_____

_____

MY RATING
⭐⭐⭐⭐⭐

New Season Begins_____

MY SHOWS

Show Title _____

Network/Streaming Service _____

Start Date _____ Day/Night/Time _____

Season # _____ Total Seasons _____

Episode Length _____ Total Episodes _____

EPISODE TRACKER

① ② ③ ④ ⑤ ⑥ ⑦ ⑧ ⑨ ⑩ ⑪ ⑫ ⑬ ⑭ ⑮ ⑯ ⑰ ⑱ ⑲ ⑳ ㉑ ㉒ ㉓ ㉔

Plot/Synopsis _____

_____

_____

_____

Notes _____

_____

_____

_____

_____

_____

_____

_____

_____

_____

MY RATING

New Season Begins _____ ★★★★★

🍿 MY SHOWS 📺

Show Title _____

Network/Streaming Service _____

Start Date _____ Day/Night/Time _____

Season # _____ Total Seasons _____

Episode Length _____ Total Episodes _____

EPISODE TRACKER

① ② ③ ④ ⑤ ⑥ ⑦ ⑧ ⑨ ⑩ ⑪ ⑫ ⑬ ⑭ ⑮ ⑯ ⑰ ⑱ ⑲ ⑳ ㉑ ㉒ ㉓ ㉔

Plot/Synopsis _____

_____

_____

Notes _____

_____

_____

_____

_____

_____

_____

_____

_____

MY RATING

⭐ ⭐ ⭐ ⭐ ⭐

New Season Begins_____

🍿 MY SHOWS 📺

Show Title _____

Network/Streaming Service _____

Start Date _____ Day/Night/Time _____

Season # _____ Total Seasons _____

Episode Length _____ Total Episodes _____

EPISODE TRACKER

① ② ③ ④ ⑤ ⑥ ⑦ ⑧ ⑨ ⑩ ⑪ ⑫ ⑬ ⑭ ⑮ ⑯ ⑰ ⑱ ⑲ ⑳ ㉑ ㉒ ㉓ ㉔

Plot/Synopsis _____

_____

_____

Notes _____

_____

_____

_____

_____

_____

_____

_____

_____

MY RATING

New Season Begins_____ ★★★★★

33

🍿 MY SHOWS 📺

Show Title _____

Network/Streaming Service _____

Start Date _____ Day/Night/Time _____

Season # _____ Total Seasons _____

Episode Length _____ Total Episodes _____

EPISODE TRACKER

①②③④⑤⑥⑦⑧⑨⑩⑪⑫⑬⑭⑮⑯⑰⑱⑲⑳㉑㉒㉓㉔

Plot/Synopsis _____

_____

_____

Notes _____

_____

_____

_____

_____

_____

_____

_____

_____

MY RATING

⭐⭐⭐⭐⭐

New Season Begins _____

MY SHOWS

Show Title _____

Network/Streaming Service _____

Start Date _____ Day/Night/Time _____

Season # _____ Total Seasons _____

Episode Length _____ Total Episodes _____

EPISODE TRACKER

① ② ③ ④ ⑤ ⑥ ⑦ ⑧ ⑨ ⑩ ⑪ ⑫ ⑬ ⑭ ⑮ ⑯ ⑰ ⑱ ⑲ ⑳ ㉑ ㉒ ㉓ ㉔

Plot/Synopsis _____

_____

_____

Notes _____

_____

_____

_____

_____

_____

_____

_____

_____

_____

MY RATING

New Season Begins _____ ★★★★★

🍿 MY SHOWS 📺

Show Title _____

Network/Streaming Service _____

Start Date _____ Day/Night/Time _____

Season # _____ Total Seasons _____

Episode Length _____ Total Episodes _____

EPISODE TRACKER

①②③④⑤⑥⑦⑧⑨⑩⑪⑫⑬⑭⑮⑯⑰⑱⑲⑳㉑㉒㉓㉔

Plot/Synopsis _____

_____

_____

Notes _____

_____

_____

_____

_____

_____

_____

_____

_____

MY RATING

_____ ⭐⭐⭐⭐⭐

New Season Begins_____

MY SHOWS

Show Title _____

Network/Streaming Service _____

Start Date _____ Day/Night/Time _____

Season # _____ Total Seasons _____

Episode Length _____ Total Episodes _____

EPISODE TRACKER

① ② ③ ④ ⑤ ⑥ ⑦ ⑧ ⑨ ⑩ ⑪ ⑫ ⑬ ⑭ ⑮ ⑯ ⑰ ⑱ ⑲ ⑳ ㉑ ㉒ ㉓ ㉔

Plot/Synopsis _____

_____

_____

Notes _____

_____

_____

_____

_____

_____

_____

_____

_____

_____

MY RATING

New Season Begins_____ ★ ★ ★ ★ ★

🍿 MY SHOWS 📺

Show Title _____

Network/Streaming Service _____

Start Date _____ Day/Night/Time _____

Season # _____ Total Seasons _____

Episode Length _____ Total Episodes _____

EPISODE TRACKER

①②③④⑤⑥⑦⑧⑨⑩⑪⑫⑬⑭⑮⑯⑰⑱⑲⑳㉑㉒㉓㉔

Plot/Synopsis _____

_____

_____

Notes _____

_____

_____

_____

_____

_____

_____

_____

_____

_____

MY RATING
⭐⭐⭐⭐⭐

New Season Begins_____

🍿 MY SHOWS 📺

Show Title _____

Network/Streaming Service _____

Start Date _____ Day/Night/Time _____

Season # _____ Total Seasons _____

Episode Length _____ Total Episodes _____

EPISODE TRACKER

① ② ③ ④ ⑤ ⑥ ⑦ ⑧ ⑨ ⑩ ⑪ ⑫ ⑬ ⑭ ⑮ ⑯ ⑰ ⑱ ⑲ ⑳ ㉑ ㉒ ㉓ ㉔

Plot/Synopsis _____

_____

_____

Notes _____

_____

_____

_____

_____

_____

_____

_____

_____

_____

_____

MY RATING

New Season Begins _____ ★★★★★

🍿 MY SHOWS 📺

Show Title _____

Network/Streaming Service _____

Start Date _____ Day/Night/Time _____

Season # _____ Total Seasons _____

Episode Length _____ Total Episodes _____

EPISODE TRACKER

① ② ③ ④ ⑤ ⑥ ⑦ ⑧ ⑨ ⑩ ⑪ ⑫ ⑬ ⑭ ⑮ ⑯ ⑰ ⑱ ⑲ ⑳ ㉑ ㉒ ㉓ ㉔

Plot/Synopsis _____

_____

_____

Notes _____

_____

_____

_____

_____

_____

_____

_____

_____

MY RATING
⭐ ⭐ ⭐ ⭐ ⭐

New Season Begins_____

🍿 MY SHOWS 📺

Show Title _____

Network/Streaming Service _____

Start Date _____ Day/Night/Time _____

Season # _____ Total Seasons _____

Episode Length _____ Total Episodes _____

EPISODE TRACKER

① ② ③ ④ ⑤ ⑥ ⑦ ⑧ ⑨ ⑩ ⑪ ⑫ ⑬ ⑭ ⑮ ⑯ ⑰ ⑱ ⑲ ⑳ ㉑ ㉒ ㉓ ㉔

Plot/Synopsis _____

_____

_____

Notes _____

_____

_____

_____

_____

_____

_____

_____

_____

MY RATING

New Season Begins_____ ⭐⭐⭐⭐⭐

🍿 MY SHOWS 📺

Show Title _____

Network/Streaming Service _____

Start Date _____ Day/Night/Time _____

Season # _____ Total Seasons _____

Episode Length _____ Total Episodes _____

EPISODE TRACKER

① ② ③ ④ ⑤ ⑥ ⑦ ⑧ ⑨ ⑩ ⑪ ⑫ ⑬ ⑭ ⑮ ⑯ ⑰ ⑱ ⑲ ⑳ ㉑ ㉒ ㉓ ㉔

Plot/Synopsis _____

_____

_____

Notes _____

_____

_____

_____

_____

_____

_____

_____

_____

_____

MY RATING

⭐ ⭐ ⭐ ⭐ ⭐

New Season Begins_____

🍿 MY SHOWS 📺

Show Title _____

Network/Streaming Service _____

Start Date _____ Day/Night/Time _____

Season # _____ Total Seasons _____

Episode Length _____ Total Episodes _____

EPISODE TRACKER

① ② ③ ④ ⑤ ⑥ ⑦ ⑧ ⑨ ⑩ ⑪ ⑫ ⑬ ⑭ ⑮ ⑯ ⑰ ⑱ ⑲ ⑳ ㉑ ㉒ ㉓ ㉔

Plot/Synopsis _____

_____

_____

Notes _____

_____

_____

_____

_____

_____

_____

_____

_____

_____

MY RATING

New Season Begins _____ ⭐⭐⭐⭐⭐

🍿 MY SHOWS 📺

Show Title _____

Network/Streaming Service _____

Start Date _____ Day/Night/Time _____

Season # _____ Total Seasons _____

Episode Length _____ Total Episodes _____

EPISODE TRACKER

①②③④⑤⑥⑦⑧⑨⑩⑪⑫⑬⑭⑮⑯⑰⑱⑲⑳㉑㉒㉓㉔

Plot/Synopsis _____

_____

_____

Notes _____

_____

_____

_____

_____

_____

_____

_____

_____

MY RATING
⭐⭐⭐⭐⭐

New Season Begins_____

🍿 MY SHOWS 📺

Show Title _____

Network/Streaming Service _____

Start Date _____ Day/Night/Time _____

Season # _____ Total Seasons _____

Episode Length _____ Total Episodes _____

EPISODE TRACKER

① ② ③ ④ ⑤ ⑥ ⑦ ⑧ ⑨ ⑩ ⑪ ⑫ ⑬ ⑭ ⑮ ⑯ ⑰ ⑱ ⑲ ⑳ ㉑ ㉒ ㉓ ㉔

Plot/Synopsis _____

_____

_____

Notes _____

_____

_____

_____

_____

_____

_____

_____

_____

_____

MY RATING

New Season Begins_____ ⭐⭐⭐⭐⭐

🍿 MY SHOWS 📺

Show Title _____

Network/Streaming Service _____

Start Date _____ Day/Night/Time _____

Season # _____ Total Seasons _____

Episode Length _____ Total Episodes _____

EPISODE TRACKER

① ② ③ ④ ⑤ ⑥ ⑦ ⑧ ⑨ ⑩ ⑪ ⑫ ⑬ ⑭ ⑮ ⑯ ⑰ ⑱ ⑲ ⑳ ㉑ ㉒ ㉓ ㉔

Plot/Synopsis _____

_____

_____

Notes _____

_____

_____

_____

_____

_____

_____

_____

_____

_____

MY RATING

⭐⭐⭐⭐⭐

New Season Begins_____

MY SHOWS

Show Title _____

Network/Streaming Service _____

Start Date _____ Day/Night/Time _____

Season # _____ Total Seasons _____

Episode Length _____ Total Episodes _____

EPISODE TRACKER

① ② ③ ④ ⑤ ⑥ ⑦ ⑧ ⑨ ⑩ ⑪ ⑫ ⑬ ⑭ ⑮ ⑯ ⑰ ⑱ ⑲ ⑳ ㉑ ㉒ ㉓ ㉔

Plot/Synopsis _____

_____

_____

Notes _____

_____

_____

_____

_____

_____

_____

_____

_____

_____

MY RATING

⭐⭐⭐⭐⭐

New Season Begins_____

🍿 MY SHOWS 📺

Show Title _____

Network/Streaming Service _____

Start Date _____ Day/Night/Time _____

Season # _____ Total Seasons _____

Episode Length _____ Total Episodes _____

EPISODE TRACKER

① ② ③ ④ ⑤ ⑥ ⑦ ⑧ ⑨ ⑩ ⑪ ⑫ ⑬ ⑭ ⑮ ⑯ ⑰ ⑱ ⑲ ⑳ ㉑ ㉒ ㉓ ㉔

Plot/Synopsis _____

_____

_____

Notes _____

_____

_____

_____

_____

_____

_____

_____

_____

_____

MY RATING

⭐ ⭐ ⭐ ⭐ ⭐

New Season Begins _____

🍿 MY SHOWS 📺

Show Title _____

Network/Streaming Service _____

Start Date _____ Day/Night/Time _____

Season # _____ Total Seasons _____

Episode Length _____ Total Episodes _____

EPISODE TRACKER

① ② ③ ④ ⑤ ⑥ ⑦ ⑧ ⑨ ⑩ ⑪ ⑫ ⑬ ⑭ ⑮ ⑯ ⑰ ⑱ ⑲ ⑳ ㉑ ㉒ ㉓ ㉔

Plot/Synopsis _____

_____

_____

Notes _____

_____

_____

_____

_____

_____

_____

_____

_____

MY RATING

⭐⭐⭐⭐⭐

New Season Begins_____

🍿 MY SHOWS 📺

Show Title _____

Network/Streaming Service _____

Start Date _____ Day/Night/Time _____

Season # _____ Total Seasons _____

Episode Length _____ Total Episodes _____

EPISODE TRACKER

① ② ③ ④ ⑤ ⑥ ⑦ ⑧ ⑨ ⑩ ⑪ ⑫ ⑬ ⑭ ⑮ ⑯ ⑰ ⑱ ⑲ ⑳ ㉑ ㉒ ㉓ ㉔

Plot/Synopsis _____

_____

_____

Notes _____

_____

_____

_____

_____

_____

_____

_____

_____

MY RATING
⭐⭐⭐⭐⭐

New Season Begins_____

MY SHOWS

Show Title _____

Network/Streaming Service _____

Start Date _____ Day/Night/Time _____

Season # _____ Total Seasons _____

Episode Length _____ Total Episodes _____

EPISODE TRACKER

① ② ③ ④ ⑤ ⑥ ⑦ ⑧ ⑨ ⑩ ⑪ ⑫ ⑬ ⑭ ⑮ ⑯ ⑰ ⑱ ⑲ ⑳ ㉑ ㉒ ㉓ ㉔

Plot/Synopsis _____

_____

_____

Notes _____

_____

_____

_____

_____

_____

_____

_____

_____

MY RATING

New Season Begins_____ ★★★★★

🍿 MY SHOWS 📺

Show Title _____

Network/Streaming Service _____

Start Date _____ Day/Night/Time _____

Season # _____ Total Seasons _____

Episode Length _____ Total Episodes _____

EPISODE TRACKER

① ② ③ ④ ⑤ ⑥ ⑦ ⑧ ⑨ ⑩ ⑪ ⑫ ⑬ ⑭ ⑮ ⑯ ⑰ ⑱ ⑲ ⑳ ㉑ ㉒ ㉓ ㉔

Plot/Synopsis _____

_____

_____

Notes _____

_____

_____

_____

_____

_____

_____

_____

_____

_____

MY RATING
⭐⭐⭐⭐⭐

New Season Begins_____

MY SHOWS

Show Title _____

Network/Streaming Service _____

Start Date _____ Day/Night/Time _____

Season # _____ Total Seasons _____

Episode Length _____ Total Episodes _____

EPISODE TRACKER

① ② ③ ④ ⑤ ⑥ ⑦ ⑧ ⑨ ⑩ ⑪ ⑫ ⑬ ⑭ ⑮ ⑯ ⑰ ⑱ ⑲ ⑳ ㉑ ㉒ ㉓ ㉔

Plot/Synopsis _____

_____

_____

Notes _____

_____

_____

_____

_____

_____

_____

_____

_____

_____

MY RATING

⭐ ⭐ ⭐ ⭐ ⭐

New Season Begins_____

🍿 MY SHOWS 📺

Show Title _____

Network/Streaming Service _____

Start Date _____ Day/Night/Time _____

Season # _____ Total Seasons _____

Episode Length _____ Total Episodes _____

EPISODE TRACKER

① ② ③ ④ ⑤ ⑥ ⑦ ⑧ ⑨ ⑩ ⑪ ⑫ ⑬ ⑭ ⑮ ⑯ ⑰ ⑱ ⑲ ⑳ ㉑ ㉒ ㉓ ㉔

Plot/Synopsis _____

_____

_____

Notes _____

_____

_____

_____

_____

_____

_____

_____

MY RATING
⭐⭐⭐⭐⭐

New Season Begins_____

🍿 MY SHOWS 📺

Show Title _____

Network/Streaming Service _____

Start Date _____ Day/Night/Time _____

Season # _____ Total Seasons _____

Episode Length _____ Total Episodes _____

EPISODE TRACKER

① ② ③ ④ ⑤ ⑥ ⑦ ⑧ ⑨ ⑩ ⑪ ⑫ ⑬ ⑭ ⑮ ⑯ ⑰ ⑱ ⑲ ⑳ ㉑ ㉒ ㉓ ㉔

Plot/Synopsis _____

_____

_____

Notes _____

_____

_____

_____

_____

_____

_____

_____

_____

_____

MY RATING

New Season Begins _____ ⭐⭐⭐⭐⭐

Show Title _____

Network/Streaming Service _____

Start Date _____ Day/Night/Time _____

Season # _____ Total Seasons _____

Episode Length _____ Total Episodes _____

EPISODE TRACKER

① ② ③ ④ ⑤ ⑥ ⑦ ⑧ ⑨ ⑩ ⑪ ⑫ ⑬ ⑭ ⑮ ⑯ ⑰ ⑱ ⑲ ⑳ ㉑ ㉒ ㉓ ㉔

Plot/Synopsis _____

_____

_____

Notes _____

_____

_____

_____

_____

_____

_____

_____

_____

MY RATING
⭐⭐⭐⭐⭐

New Season Begins_____

🍿 MY SHOWS 📺

Show Title _____

Network/Streaming Service _____

Start Date _____ Day/Night/Time _____

Season # _____ Total Seasons _____

Episode Length _____ Total Episodes _____

EPISODE TRACKER

① ② ③ ④ ⑤ ⑥ ⑦ ⑧ ⑨ ⑩ ⑪ ⑫ ⑬ ⑭ ⑮ ⑯ ⑰ ⑱ ⑲ ⑳ ㉑ ㉒ ㉓ ㉔

Plot/Synopsis _____

_____

_____

Notes _____

_____

_____

_____

_____

_____

_____

_____

_____

_____ **MY RATING**

New Season Begins_____ ⭐⭐⭐⭐⭐

🍿 MY SHOWS 📺

Show Title _____

Network/Streaming Service _____

Start Date _____ Day/Night/Time _____

Season # _____ Total Seasons _____

Episode Length _____ Total Episodes _____

EPISODE TRACKER

① ② ③ ④ ⑤ ⑥ ⑦ ⑧ ⑨ ⑩ ⑪ ⑫ ⑬ ⑭ ⑮ ⑯ ⑰ ⑱ ⑲ ⑳ ㉑ ㉒ ㉓ ㉔

Plot/Synopsis _____

_____

_____

Notes _____

_____

_____

_____

_____

_____

_____

_____

MY RATING

⭐⭐⭐⭐⭐

New Season Begins_____

MY SHOWS

Show Title _____

Network/Streaming Service _____

Start Date _____ Day/Night/Time _____

Season # _____ Total Seasons _____

Episode Length _____ Total Episodes _____

EPISODE TRACKER

① ② ③ ④ ⑤ ⑥ ⑦ ⑧ ⑨ ⑩ ⑪ ⑫ ⑬ ⑭ ⑮ ⑯ ⑰ ⑱ ⑲ ⑳ ㉑ ㉒ ㉓ ㉔

Plot/Synopsis _____

_____

_____

Notes _____

_____

_____

_____

_____

_____

_____

_____

_____

MY RATING

New Season Begins_____ ★★★★★

🍿 MY SHOWS 📺

Show Title _____

Network/Streaming Service _____

Start Date _____ Day/Night/Time _____

Season # _____ Total Seasons _____

Episode Length _____ Total Episodes _____

EPISODE TRACKER

① ② ③ ④ ⑤ ⑥ ⑦ ⑧ ⑨ ⑩ ⑪ ⑫ ⑬ ⑭ ⑮ ⑯ ⑰ ⑱ ⑲ ⑳ ㉑ ㉒ ㉓ ㉔

Plot/Synopsis _____

_____

_____

Notes _____

_____

_____

_____

_____

_____

_____

_____

_____

_____

MY RATING
⭐⭐⭐⭐⭐

New Season Begins_____

🍿 MY SHOWS 📺

Show Title _____

Network/Streaming Service _____

Start Date _____ Day/Night/Time _____

Season # _____ Total Seasons _____

Episode Length _____ Total Episodes _____

EPISODE TRACKER

①②③④⑤⑥⑦⑧⑨⑩⑪⑫⑬⑭⑮⑯⑰⑱⑲⑳㉑㉒㉓㉔

Plot/Synopsis _____

_____

_____

Notes _____

_____

_____

_____

_____

_____

_____

_____

_____

_____

MY RATING

New Season Begins_____ ★★★★★

🍿 MY SHOWS 📺

Show Title _____

Network/Streaming Service _____

Start Date _____ Day/Night/Time _____

Season # _____ Total Seasons _____

Episode Length _____ Total Episodes _____

EPISODE TRACKER

① ② ③ ④ ⑤ ⑥ ⑦ ⑧ ⑨ ⑩ ⑪ ⑫ ⑬ ⑭ ⑮ ⑯ ⑰ ⑱ ⑲ ⑳ ㉑ ㉒ ㉓ ㉔

Plot/Synopsis _____

_____

_____

Notes _____

_____

_____

_____

_____

_____

_____

_____

_____

MY RATING
⭐⭐⭐⭐⭐

New Season Begins_____

MY SHOWS

Show Title _____

Network/Streaming Service _____

Start Date _____ Day/Night/Time _____

Season # _____ Total Seasons _____

Episode Length _____ Total Episodes _____

EPISODE TRACKER

① ② ③ ④ ⑤ ⑥ ⑦ ⑧ ⑨ ⑩ ⑪ ⑫ ⑬ ⑭ ⑮ ⑯ ⑰ ⑱ ⑲ ⑳ ㉑ ㉒ ㉓ ㉔

Plot/Synopsis _____

_____

_____

Notes _____

_____

_____

_____

_____

_____

_____

_____

_____

_____

MY RATING
⭐⭐⭐⭐⭐

New Season Begins_____

🍿 MY SHOWS 📺

Show Title _____

Network/Streaming Service _____

Start Date _____ Day/Night/Time _____

Season # _____ Total Seasons _____

Episode Length _____ Total Episodes _____

EPISODE TRACKER

① ② ③ ④ ⑤ ⑥ ⑦ ⑧ ⑨ ⑩ ⑪ ⑫ ⑬ ⑭ ⑮ ⑯ ⑰ ⑱ ⑲ ⑳ ㉑ ㉒ ㉓ ㉔

Plot/Synopsis _____

_____

_____

Notes _____

_____

_____

_____

_____

_____

_____

_____

_____

MY RATING

⭐⭐⭐⭐⭐

New Season Begins _____

 MY SHOWS

Show Title _____

Network/Streaming Service _____

Start Date _____ Day/Night/Time _____

Season # _____ Total Seasons _____

Episode Length _____ Total Episodes _____

EPISODE TRACKER

① ② ③ ④ ⑤ ⑥ ⑦ ⑧ ⑨ ⑩ ⑪ ⑫ ⑬ ⑭ ⑮ ⑯ ⑰ ⑱ ⑲ ⑳ ㉑ ㉒ ㉓ ㉔

Plot/Synopsis _____

_____

_____

_____

Notes _____

_____

_____

_____

_____

_____

_____

_____

_____

MY RATING

New Season Begins_____ ★★★★★

🍿 MY SHOWS 📺

Show Title _____

Network/Streaming Service _____

Start Date _____ Day/Night/Time _____

Season # _____ Total Seasons _____

Episode Length _____ Total Episodes _____

EPISODE TRACKER

① ② ③ ④ ⑤ ⑥ ⑦ ⑧ ⑨ ⑩ ⑪ ⑫ ⑬ ⑭ ⑮ ⑯ ⑰ ⑱ ⑲ ⑳ ㉑ ㉒ ㉓ ㉔

Plot/Synopsis _____

_____

_____

Notes _____

_____

_____

_____

_____

_____

_____

_____

_____

_____

MY RATING
⭐⭐⭐⭐⭐

New Season Begins _____

MY SHOWS

Show Title _____

Network/Streaming Service _____

Start Date _____ Day/Night/Time _____

Season # _____ Total Seasons _____

Episode Length _____ Total Episodes _____

EPISODE TRACKER

① ② ③ ④ ⑤ ⑥ ⑦ ⑧ ⑨ ⑩ ⑪ ⑫ ⑬ ⑭ ⑮ ⑯ ⑰ ⑱ ⑲ ⑳ ㉑ ㉒ ㉓ ㉔

Plot/Synopsis _____

_____

_____

Notes _____

_____

_____

_____

_____

_____

_____

_____

_____

MY RATING

New Season Begins_____ ★★★★★

🍿 MY SHOWS 📺

Show Title _____

Network/Streaming Service _____

Start Date _____ Day/Night/Time _____

Season # _____ Total Seasons _____

Episode Length _____ Total Episodes _____

EPISODE TRACKER

① ② ③ ④ ⑤ ⑥ ⑦ ⑧ ⑨ ⑩ ⑪ ⑫ ⑬ ⑭ ⑮ ⑯ ⑰ ⑱ ⑲ ⑳ ㉑ ㉒ ㉓ ㉔

Plot/Synopsis _____

_____

_____

Notes _____

_____

_____

_____

_____

_____

_____

_____

_____

_____

MY RATING
⭐⭐⭐⭐⭐

New Season Begins _____

MY SHOWS

Show Title _____

Network/Streaming Service _____

Start Date _____ Day/Night/Time _____

Season # _____ Total Seasons _____

Episode Length _____ Total Episodes _____

EPISODE TRACKER

①②③④⑤⑥⑦⑧⑨⑩⑪⑫⑬⑭⑮⑯⑰⑱⑲⑳㉑㉒㉓㉔

Plot/Synopsis _____

_____

_____

_____

Notes _____

_____

_____

_____

_____

_____

_____

_____

_____

_____

MY RATING

New Season Begins _____ ★★★★★

🍿 MY SHOWS 📺

Show Title _____

Network/Streaming Service _____

Start Date _____ Day/Night/Time _____

Season # _____ Total Seasons _____

Episode Length _____ Total Episodes _____

EPISODE TRACKER

① ② ③ ④ ⑤ ⑥ ⑦ ⑧ ⑨ ⑩ ⑪ ⑫ ⑬ ⑭ ⑮ ⑯ ⑰ ⑱ ⑲ ⑳ ㉑ ㉒ ㉓ ㉔

Plot/Synopsis _____

_____

_____

Notes _____

_____

_____

_____

_____

_____

_____

_____

_____

_____

MY RATING
⭐⭐⭐⭐⭐

New Season Begins_____

🍿 MY SHOWS 📺

Show Title _____

Network/Streaming Service _____

Start Date _____ Day/Night/Time _____

Season # _____ Total Seasons _____

Episode Length _____ Total Episodes _____

EPISODE TRACKER

① ② ③ ④ ⑤ ⑥ ⑦ ⑧ ⑨ ⑩ ⑪ ⑫ ⑬ ⑭ ⑮ ⑯ ⑰ ⑱ ⑲ ⑳ ㉑ ㉒ ㉓ ㉔

Plot/Synopsis _____

_____

_____

Notes _____

_____

_____

_____

_____

_____

_____

_____

_____

_____

_____

New Season Begins _____

MY RATING
⭐⭐⭐⭐⭐

🍿 MY SHOWS 📺

Show Title _____

Network/Streaming Service _____

Start Date _____ Day/Night/Time _____

Season # _____ Total Seasons _____

Episode Length _____ Total Episodes _____

EPISODE TRACKER

①②③④⑤⑥⑦⑧⑨⑩⑪⑫⑬⑭⑮⑯⑰⑱⑲⑳㉑㉒㉓㉔

Plot/Synopsis _____

_____

_____

Notes _____

_____

_____

_____

_____

_____

_____

_____

_____

_____

_____

MY RATING
⭐⭐⭐⭐⭐

New Season Begins_____

🍿 MY SHOWS 📺

Show Title _____

Network/Streaming Service _____

Start Date _____ Day/Night/Time _____

Season # _____ Total Seasons _____

Episode Length _____ Total Episodes _____

EPISODE TRACKER

①②③④⑤⑥⑦⑧⑨⑩⑪⑫⑬⑭⑮⑯⑰⑱⑲⑳㉑㉒㉓㉔

Plot/Synopsis _____

_____

_____

Notes _____

_____

_____

_____

_____

_____

_____

_____

_____

_____

MY RATING

New Season Begins_____ ⭐⭐⭐⭐⭐

🍿 MY SHOWS 📺

Show Title _____

Network/Streaming Service _____

Start Date _____ Day/Night/Time _____

Season # _____ Total Seasons _____

Episode Length _____ Total Episodes _____

EPISODE TRACKER

① ② ③ ④ ⑤ ⑥ ⑦ ⑧ ⑨ ⑩ ⑪ ⑫ ⑬ ⑭ ⑮ ⑯ ⑰ ⑱ ⑲ ⑳ ㉑ ㉒ ㉓ ㉔

Plot/Synopsis _____

_____

_____

Notes _____

_____

_____

_____

_____

_____

_____

_____

_____

MY RATING
⭐⭐⭐⭐⭐

New Season Begins_____

74

MY SHOWS

Show Title _____

Network/Streaming Service _____

Start Date _____ Day/Night/Time _____

Season # _____ Total Seasons _____

Episode Length _____ Total Episodes _____

EPISODE TRACKER

① ② ③ ④ ⑤ ⑥ ⑦ ⑧ ⑨ ⑩ ⑪ ⑫ ⑬ ⑭ ⑮ ⑯ ⑰ ⑱ ⑲ ⑳ ㉑ ㉒ ㉓ ㉔

Plot/Synopsis _____

_____

_____

Notes _____

_____

_____

_____

_____

_____

_____

_____

_____

_____

MY RATING

New Season Begins _____ ★★★★★

🍿 MY SHOWS 📺

Show Title _____

Network/Streaming Service _____

Start Date _____ Day/Night/Time _____

Season # _____ Total Seasons _____

Episode Length _____ Total Episodes _____

EPISODE TRACKER

① ② ③ ④ ⑤ ⑥ ⑦ ⑧ ⑨ ⑩ ⑪ ⑫ ⑬ ⑭ ⑮ ⑯ ⑰ ⑱ ⑲ ⑳ ㉑ ㉒ ㉓ ㉔

Plot/Synopsis _____

_____

_____

Notes _____

_____

_____

_____

_____

_____

_____

_____

_____

MY RATING
⭐⭐⭐⭐⭐

New Season Begins_____

MY SHOWS

Show Title _____

Network/Streaming Service _____

Start Date _____ Day/Night/Time _____

Season # _____ Total Seasons _____

Episode Length _____ Total Episodes _____

EPISODE TRACKER

① ② ③ ④ ⑤ ⑥ ⑦ ⑧ ⑨ ⑩ ⑪ ⑫ ⑬ ⑭ ⑮ ⑯ ⑰ ⑱ ⑲ ⑳ ㉑ ㉒ ㉓ ㉔

Plot/Synopsis _____

_____

_____

Notes _____

_____

_____

_____

_____

_____

_____

_____

_____

_____

MY RATING

New Season Begins_____ ★★★★★

77

🍿 MY SHOWS 📺

Show Title _____

Network/Streaming Service _____

Start Date _____ Day/Night/Time _____

Season # _____ Total Seasons _____

Episode Length _____ Total Episodes _____

EPISODE TRACKER

①②③④⑤⑥⑦⑧⑨⑩⑪⑫⑬⑭⑮⑯⑰⑱⑲⑳㉑㉒㉓㉔

Plot/Synopsis _____

_____

_____

Notes _____

_____

_____

_____

_____

_____

_____

_____

_____

MY RATING

New Season Begins_____ ⭐⭐⭐⭐⭐

MY SHOWS

Show Title _____

Network/Streaming Service _____

Start Date _____ Day/Night/Time _____

Season # _____ Total Seasons _____

Episode Length _____ Total Episodes _____

EPISODE TRACKER

① ② ③ ④ ⑤ ⑥ ⑦ ⑧ ⑨ ⑩ ⑪ ⑫ ⑬ ⑭ ⑮ ⑯ ⑰ ⑱ ⑲ ⑳ ㉑ ㉒ ㉓ ㉔

Plot/Synopsis _____

_____

_____

Notes _____

_____

_____

_____

_____

_____

_____

_____

_____

_____

MY RATING

New Season Begins_____ ★★★★★

79

🍿 MY SHOWS 📺

Show Title _____

Network/Streaming Service _____

Start Date _____ Day/Night/Time _____

Season # _____ Total Seasons _____

Episode Length _____ Total Episodes _____

EPISODE TRACKER

① ② ③ ④ ⑤ ⑥ ⑦ ⑧ ⑨ ⑩ ⑪ ⑫ ⑬ ⑭ ⑮ ⑯ ⑰ ⑱ ⑲ ⑳ ㉑ ㉒ ㉓ ㉔

Plot/Synopsis _____

_____

_____

Notes _____

_____

_____

_____

_____

_____

_____

_____

_____

_____

MY RATING

New Season Begins _____ ★★★★★

🍿 MY SHOWS 📺

Show Title _____

Network/Streaming Service _____

Start Date _____ Day/Night/Time _____

Season # _____ Total Seasons _____

Episode Length _____ Total Episodes _____

EPISODE TRACKER

① ② ③ ④ ⑤ ⑥ ⑦ ⑧ ⑨ ⑩ ⑪ ⑫ ⑬ ⑭ ⑮ ⑯ ⑰ ⑱ ⑲ ⑳ ㉑ ㉒ ㉓ ㉔

Plot/Synopsis _____

_____

_____

Notes _____

_____

_____

_____

_____

_____

_____

_____

_____

_____

MY RATING

⭐⭐⭐⭐⭐

New Season Begins_____

🍿 MY SHOWS 📺

Show Title _____

Network/Streaming Service _____

Start Date _____ Day/Night/Time _____

Season # _____ Total Seasons _____

Episode Length _____ Total Episodes _____

EPISODE TRACKER

① ② ③ ④ ⑤ ⑥ ⑦ ⑧ ⑨ ⑩ ⑪ ⑫ ⑬ ⑭ ⑮ ⑯ ⑰ ⑱ ⑲ ⑳ ㉑ ㉒ ㉓ ㉔

Plot/Synopsis _____

_____

_____

Notes _____

_____

_____

_____

_____

_____

_____

_____

_____

MY RATING
⭐⭐⭐⭐⭐

New Season Begins_____

MY SHOWS

Show Title _____

Network/Streaming Service _____

Start Date _____ Day/Night/Time _____

Season # _____ Total Seasons _____

Episode Length _____ Total Episodes _____

EPISODE TRACKER

① ② ③ ④ ⑤ ⑥ ⑦ ⑧ ⑨ ⑩ ⑪ ⑫ ⑬ ⑭ ⑮ ⑯ ⑰ ⑱ ⑲ ⑳ ㉑ ㉒ ㉓ ㉔

Plot/Synopsis _____

_____

_____

Notes _____

_____

_____

_____

_____

_____

_____

_____

_____

_____

MY RATING

New Season Begins_____ ★ ★ ★ ★ ★

83

🍿 MY SHOWS 📺

Show Title _____

Network/Streaming Service _____

Start Date _____ Day/Night/Time _____

Season # _____ Total Seasons _____

Episode Length _____ Total Episodes _____

EPISODE TRACKER

① ② ③ ④ ⑤ ⑥ ⑦ ⑧ ⑨ ⑩ ⑪ ⑫ ⑬ ⑭ ⑮ ⑯ ⑰ ⑱ ⑲ ⑳ ㉑ ㉒ ㉓ ㉔

Plot/Synopsis _____

_____

_____

Notes _____

_____

_____

_____

_____

_____

_____

_____

_____

_____

MY RATING

⭐⭐⭐⭐⭐

New Season Begins_____

🍿 MY SHOWS 🎞

Show Title _____

Network/Streaming Service _____

Start Date _____ Day/Night/Time _____

Season # _____ Total Seasons _____

Episode Length _____ Total Episodes _____

EPISODE TRACKER

① ② ③ ④ ⑤ ⑥ ⑦ ⑧ ⑨ ⑩ ⑪ ⑫ ⑬ ⑭ ⑮ ⑯ ⑰ ⑱ ⑲ ⑳ ㉑ ㉒ ㉓ ㉔

Plot/Synopsis _____

_____

_____

Notes _____

_____

_____

_____

_____

_____

_____

_____

_____

_____

MY RATING

New Season Begins_____ ★★★★★

85

🍿 MY SHOWS 📺

Show Title _____

Network/Streaming Service _____

Start Date _____ Day/Night/Time _____

Season # _____ Total Seasons _____

Episode Length _____ Total Episodes _____

EPISODE TRACKER

① ② ③ ④ ⑤ ⑥ ⑦ ⑧ ⑨ ⑩ ⑪ ⑫ ⑬ ⑭ ⑮ ⑯ ⑰ ⑱ ⑲ ⑳ ㉑ ㉒ ㉓ ㉔

Plot/Synopsis _____

_____

_____

Notes _____

_____

_____

_____

_____

_____

_____

_____

MY RATING
★★★★★

New Season Begins_____

🍿 MY SHOWS 📺

Show Title _____

Network/Streaming Service _____

Start Date _____ Day/Night/Time _____

Season # _____ Total Seasons _____

Episode Length _____ Total Episodes _____

EPISODE TRACKER
①②③④⑤⑥⑦⑧⑨⑩⑪⑫⑬⑭⑮⑯⑰⑱⑲⑳㉑㉒㉓㉔

Plot/Synopsis _____

_____

_____

Notes _____

_____

_____

_____

_____

_____

_____

_____

_____

MY RATING

New Season Begins_____ ⭐⭐⭐⭐⭐

87

🍿 MY SHOWS 📺

Show Title _____

Network/Streaming Service _____

Start Date _____ Day/Night/Time _____

Season # _____ Total Seasons _____

Episode Length _____ Total Episodes _____

EPISODE TRACKER

① ② ③ ④ ⑤ ⑥ ⑦ ⑧ ⑨ ⑩ ⑪ ⑫ ⑬ ⑭ ⑮ ⑯ ⑰ ⑱ ⑲ ⑳ ㉑ ㉒ ㉓ ㉔

Plot/Synopsis _____

_____

_____

Notes _____

_____

_____

_____

_____

_____

_____

_____

_____

_____

MY RATING

⭐ ⭐ ⭐ ⭐ ⭐

New Season Begins_____

🍿 MY SHOWS 📺

Show Title _____

Network/Streaming Service _____

Start Date _____ Day/Night/Time _____

Season # _____ Total Seasons _____

Episode Length _____ Total Episodes _____

EPISODE TRACKER

① ② ③ ④ ⑤ ⑥ ⑦ ⑧ ⑨ ⑩ ⑪ ⑫ ⑬ ⑭ ⑮ ⑯ ⑰ ⑱ ⑲ ⑳ ㉑ ㉒ ㉓ ㉔

Plot/Synopsis _____

_____

_____

Notes _____

_____

_____

_____

_____

_____

_____

_____

_____

_____

MY RATING

⭐⭐⭐⭐⭐

New Season Begins_____

🍿 MY SHOWS 📺

Show Title _____

Network/Streaming Service _____

Start Date _____ Day/Night/Time _____

Season # _____ Total Seasons _____

Episode Length _____ Total Episodes _____

EPISODE TRACKER

①②③④⑤⑥⑦⑧⑨⑩⑪⑫⑬⑭⑮⑯⑰⑱⑲⑳㉑㉒㉓㉔

Plot/Synopsis _____

_____

_____

Notes _____

_____

_____

_____

_____

_____

_____

_____

_____

MY RATING

⭐⭐⭐⭐⭐

New Season Begins_____

MY SHOWS

Show Title _____

Network/Streaming Service _____

Start Date _____ Day/Night/Time _____

Season # _____ Total Seasons _____

Episode Length _____ Total Episodes _____

EPISODE TRACKER

① ② ③ ④ ⑤ ⑥ ⑦ ⑧ ⑨ ⑩ ⑪ ⑫ ⑬ ⑭ ⑮ ⑯ ⑰ ⑱ ⑲ ⑳ ㉑ ㉒ ㉓ ㉔

Plot/Synopsis _____

_____

_____

Notes _____

_____

_____

_____

_____

_____

_____

_____

_____

_____

MY RATING
★ ★ ★ ★ ★

New Season Begins_____

🍿 MY SHOWS 📺

Show Title _____

Network/Streaming Service _____

Start Date _____ Day/Night/Time _____

Season # _____ Total Seasons _____

Episode Length _____ Total Episodes _____

EPISODE TRACKER

① ② ③ ④ ⑤ ⑥ ⑦ ⑧ ⑨ ⑩ ⑪ ⑫ ⑬ ⑭ ⑮ ⑯ ⑰ ⑱ ⑲ ⑳ ㉑ ㉒ ㉓ ㉔

Plot/Synopsis _____

_____

_____

Notes _____

_____

_____

_____

_____

_____

_____

_____

_____

MY RATING
⭐ ⭐ ⭐ ⭐ ⭐

New Season Begins_____

🍿 MY SHOWS 📺

Show Title _____

Network/Streaming Service _____

Start Date _____ Day/Night/Time _____

Season # _____ Total Seasons _____

Episode Length _____ Total Episodes _____

EPISODE TRACKER

① ② ③ ④ ⑤ ⑥ ⑦ ⑧ ⑨ ⑩ ⑪ ⑫ ⑬ ⑭ ⑮ ⑯ ⑰ ⑱ ⑲ ⑳ ㉑ ㉒ ㉓ ㉔

Plot/Synopsis _____

_____

_____

Notes _____

_____

_____

_____

_____

_____

_____

_____

_____

MY RATING

New Season Begins_____ ★★★★★

🍿 MY SHOWS 📺

Show Title _____

Network/Streaming Service _____

Start Date _____ Day/Night/Time _____

Season # _____ Total Seasons _____

Episode Length _____ Total Episodes _____

EPISODE TRACKER

① ② ③ ④ ⑤ ⑥ ⑦ ⑧ ⑨ ⑩ ⑪ ⑫ ⑬ ⑭ ⑮ ⑯ ⑰ ⑱ ⑲ ⑳ ㉑ ㉒ ㉓ ㉔

Plot/Synopsis _____

_____

_____

Notes _____

_____

_____

_____

_____

_____

_____

_____

_____

_____

MY RATING
⭐⭐⭐⭐⭐

New Season Begins_____

MY SHOWS

Show Title _____

Network/Streaming Service _____

Start Date _____ Day/Night/Time _____

Season # _____ Total Seasons _____

Episode Length _____ Total Episodes _____

EPISODE TRACKER

① ② ③ ④ ⑤ ⑥ ⑦ ⑧ ⑨ ⑩ ⑪ ⑫ ⑬ ⑭ ⑮ ⑯ ⑰ ⑱ ⑲ ⑳ ㉑ ㉒ ㉓ ㉔

Plot/Synopsis _____

_____

_____

Notes _____

_____

_____

_____

_____

_____

_____

_____

_____

_____

MY RATING
★★★★★

New Season Begins_____

🍿 MY SHOWS 📺

Show Title _____

Network/Streaming Service _____

Start Date _____ Day/Night/Time _____

Season # _____ Total Seasons _____

Episode Length _____ Total Episodes _____

EPISODE TRACKER

① ② ③ ④ ⑤ ⑥ ⑦ ⑧ ⑨ ⑩ ⑪ ⑫ ⑬ ⑭ ⑮ ⑯ ⑰ ⑱ ⑲ ⑳ ㉑ ㉒ ㉓ ㉔

Plot/Synopsis _____

_____

_____

Notes _____

_____

_____

_____

_____

_____

_____

_____

_____

_____

MY RATING

New Season Begins _____ ⭐⭐⭐⭐⭐

🍿 MY SHOWS 📺

Show Title _____

Network/Streaming Service _____

Start Date _____ Day/Night/Time _____

Season # _____ Total Seasons _____

Episode Length _____ Total Episodes _____

EPISODE TRACKER

① ② ③ ④ ⑤ ⑥ ⑦ ⑧ ⑨ ⑩ ⑪ ⑫ ⑬ ⑭ ⑮ ⑯ ⑰ ⑱ ⑲ ⑳ ㉑ ㉒ ㉓ ㉔

Plot/Synopsis _____

_____

_____

Notes _____

_____

_____

_____

_____

_____

_____

_____

_____

MY RATING

New Season Begins _____ ⭐⭐⭐⭐⭐

🍿 MY SHOWS 📺

Show Title _____

Network/Streaming Service _____

Start Date _____ Day/Night/Time _____

Season # _____ Total Seasons _____

Episode Length _____ Total Episodes _____

EPISODE TRACKER

① ② ③ ④ ⑤ ⑥ ⑦ ⑧ ⑨ ⑩ ⑪ ⑫ ⑬ ⑭ ⑮ ⑯ ⑰ ⑱ ⑲ ⑳ ㉑ ㉒ ㉓ ㉔

Plot/Synopsis _____

_____

_____

Notes _____

_____

_____

_____

_____

_____

_____

_____

_____

_____

MY RATING
⭐⭐⭐⭐⭐

New Season Begins_____

🍿 MY SHOWS 📺

Show Title _____

Network/Streaming Service _____

Start Date _____ Day/Night/Time _____

Season # _____ Total Seasons _____

Episode Length _____ Total Episodes _____

EPISODE TRACKER

① ② ③ ④ ⑤ ⑥ ⑦ ⑧ ⑨ ⑩ ⑪ ⑫ ⑬ ⑭ ⑮ ⑯ ⑰ ⑱ ⑲ ⑳ ㉑ ㉒ ㉓ ㉔

Plot/Synopsis _____

_____

_____

Notes _____

_____

_____

_____

_____

_____

_____

_____

_____

_____

MY RATING

New Season Begins _____ ⭐⭐⭐⭐⭐

🍿 MY SHOWS 📺

Show Title _____

Network/Streaming Service _____

Start Date _____ Day/Night/Time _____

Season # _____ Total Seasons _____

Episode Length _____ Total Episodes _____

EPISODE TRACKER

① ② ③ ④ ⑤ ⑥ ⑦ ⑧ ⑨ ⑩ ⑪ ⑫ ⑬ ⑭ ⑮ ⑯ ⑰ ⑱ ⑲ ⑳ ㉑ ㉒ ㉓ ㉔

Plot/Synopsis _____

_____

_____

Notes _____

_____

_____

_____

_____

_____

_____

_____

MY RATING
⭐⭐⭐⭐⭐

New Season Begins _____

🍿 MY SHOWS 📺

Show Title _____

Network/Streaming Service _____

Start Date _____ Day/Night/Time _____

Season # _____ Total Seasons _____

Episode Length _____ Total Episodes _____

EPISODE TRACKER

① ② ③ ④ ⑤ ⑥ ⑦ ⑧ ⑨ ⑩ ⑪ ⑫ ⑬ ⑭ ⑮ ⑯ ⑰ ⑱ ⑲ ⑳ ㉑ ㉒ ㉓ ㉔

Plot/Synopsis _____

_____

_____

Notes _____

_____

_____

_____

_____

_____

_____

_____

_____

_____

MY RATING
⭐⭐⭐⭐⭐

New Season Begins_____

🍿 MY SHOWS 📺

Show Title _____

Network/Streaming Service _____

Start Date _____ Day/Night/Time _____

Season # _____ Total Seasons _____

Episode Length _____ Total Episodes _____

EPISODE TRACKER

① ② ③ ④ ⑤ ⑥ ⑦ ⑧ ⑨ ⑩ ⑪ ⑫ ⑬ ⑭ ⑮ ⑯ ⑰ ⑱ ⑲ ⑳ ㉑ ㉒ ㉓ ㉔

Plot/Synopsis _____

_____

_____

Notes _____

_____

_____

_____

_____

_____

_____

_____

_____

_____

MY RATING
⭐⭐⭐⭐⭐

New Season Begins_____

🍿 MY SHOWS 📺

Show Title _____

Network/Streaming Service _____

Start Date _____ Day/Night/Time _____

Season # _____ Total Seasons _____

Episode Length _____ Total Episodes _____

EPISODE TRACKER

① ② ③ ④ ⑤ ⑥ ⑦ ⑧ ⑨ ⑩ ⑪ ⑫ ⑬ ⑭ ⑮ ⑯ ⑰ ⑱ ⑲ ⑳ ㉑ ㉒ ㉓ ㉔

Plot/Synopsis _____

_____

_____

Notes _____

_____

_____

_____

_____

_____

_____

_____

_____

MY RATING

New Season Begins _____ ★ ★ ★ ★ ★

🍿 MY SHOWS 📺

Show Title _____

Network/Streaming Service _____

Start Date _____ Day/Night/Time _____

Season # _____ Total Seasons _____

Episode Length _____ Total Episodes _____

EPISODE TRACKER

① ② ③ ④ ⑤ ⑥ ⑦ ⑧ ⑨ ⑩ ⑪ ⑫ ⑬ ⑭ ⑮ ⑯ ⑰ ⑱ ⑲ ⑳ ㉑ ㉒ ㉓ ㉔

Plot/Synopsis _____

_____

_____

Notes _____

_____

_____

_____

_____

_____

_____

_____

_____

MY RATING
⭐⭐⭐⭐⭐

New Season Begins_____

🍿 MY SHOWS 📺

Show Title _____

Network/Streaming Service _____

Start Date _____ Day/Night/Time _____

Season # _____ Total Seasons _____

Episode Length _____ Total Episodes _____

EPISODE TRACKER

① ② ③ ④ ⑤ ⑥ ⑦ ⑧ ⑨ ⑩ ⑪ ⑫ ⑬ ⑭ ⑮ ⑯ ⑰ ⑱ ⑲ ⑳ ㉑ ㉒ ㉓ ㉔

Plot/Synopsis _____

_____

_____

Notes _____

_____

_____

_____

_____

_____

_____

_____

_____

_____

_____

MY RATING

⭐ ⭐ ⭐ ⭐ ⭐

New Season Begins _____

Show Title _____

Network/Streaming Service _____

Start Date _____ Day/Night/Time _____

Season # _____ Total Seasons _____

Episode Length _____ Total Episodes _____

EPISODE TRACKER

① ② ③ ④ ⑤ ⑥ ⑦ ⑧ ⑨ ⑩ ⑪ ⑫ ⑬ ⑭ ⑮ ⑯ ⑰ ⑱ ⑲ ⑳ ㉑ ㉒ ㉓ ㉔

Plot/Synopsis _____

_____

_____

Notes _____

_____

_____

_____

_____

_____

_____

_____

MY RATING

⭐⭐⭐⭐⭐

New Season Begins_____

🍿 MY SHOWS 📺

Show Title _____

Network/Streaming Service _____

Start Date _____ Day/Night/Time _____

Season # _____ Total Seasons _____

Episode Length _____ Total Episodes _____

EPISODE TRACKER

① ② ③ ④ ⑤ ⑥ ⑦ ⑧ ⑨ ⑩ ⑪ ⑫ ⑬ ⑭ ⑮ ⑯ ⑰ ⑱ ⑲ ⑳ ㉑ ㉒ ㉓ ㉔

Plot/Synopsis _____

_____

_____

Notes _____

_____

_____

_____

_____

_____

_____

_____

_____

_____

MY RATING

New Season Begins _____ ⭐⭐⭐⭐⭐

Show Title _____

Network/Streaming Service _____

Start Date _____ Day/Night/Time _____

Season # _____ Total Seasons _____

Episode Length _____ Total Episodes _____

EPISODE TRACKER

① ② ③ ④ ⑤ ⑥ ⑦ ⑧ ⑨ ⑩ ⑪ ⑫ ⑬ ⑭ ⑮ ⑯ ⑰ ⑱ ⑲ ⑳ ㉑ ㉒ ㉓ ㉔

Plot/Synopsis _____

_____

_____

Notes _____

_____

_____

_____

_____

_____

_____

_____

_____

MY RATING
⭐⭐⭐⭐⭐

New Season Begins_____

🍿 MY SHOWS 📺

Show Title _____

Network/Streaming Service _____

Start Date _____ Day/Night/Time _____

Season # _____ Total Seasons _____

Episode Length _____ Total Episodes _____

EPISODE TRACKER

① ② ③ ④ ⑤ ⑥ ⑦ ⑧ ⑨ ⑩ ⑪ ⑫ ⑬ ⑭ ⑮ ⑯ ⑰ ⑱ ⑲ ⑳ ㉑ ㉒ ㉓ ㉔

Plot/Synopsis _____

_____

_____

Notes _____

_____

_____

_____

_____

_____

_____

_____

_____

_____

MY RATING

New Season Begins _____ ⭐⭐⭐⭐⭐

🍿 MY SHOWS 📺

Show Title _____

Network/Streaming Service _____

Start Date _____ Day/Night/Time _____

Season # _____ Total Seasons _____

Episode Length _____ Total Episodes _____

EPISODE TRACKER

①②③④⑤⑥⑦⑧⑨⑩⑪⑫⑬⑭⑮⑯⑰⑱⑲⑳㉑㉒㉓㉔

Plot/Synopsis _____

_____

_____

Notes _____

_____

_____

_____

_____

_____

_____

_____

_____

MY RATING
⭐⭐⭐⭐⭐

New Season Begins_____

🍿 MY SHOWS 📺

Show Title _____

Network/Streaming Service _____

Start Date _____ Day/Night/Time _____

Season # _____ Total Seasons _____

Episode Length _____ Total Episodes _____

EPISODE TRACKER

① ② ③ ④ ⑤ ⑥ ⑦ ⑧ ⑨ ⑩ ⑪ ⑫ ⑬ ⑭ ⑮ ⑯ ⑰ ⑱ ⑲ ⑳ ㉑ ㉒ ㉓ ㉔

Plot/Synopsis _____

_____

_____

Notes _____

_____

_____

_____

_____

_____

_____

_____

_____

MY RATING
⭐ ⭐ ⭐ ⭐ ⭐

New Season Begins_____

🍿 MY SHOWS 📺

Show Title _____

Network/Streaming Service _____

Start Date _____ Day/Night/Time _____

Season # _____ Total Seasons _____

Episode Length _____ Total Episodes _____

EPISODE TRACKER

① ② ③ ④ ⑤ ⑥ ⑦ ⑧ ⑨ ⑩ ⑪ ⑫ ⑬ ⑭ ⑮ ⑯ ⑰ ⑱ ⑲ ⑳ ㉑ ㉒ ㉓ ㉔

Plot/Synopsis _____

_____

_____

Notes _____

_____

_____

_____

_____

_____

_____

_____

_____

MY RATING
⭐⭐⭐⭐⭐

New Season Begins_____

Show Title _____

Network/Streaming Service _____

Start Date _____ Day/Night/Time _____

Season # _____ Total Seasons _____

Episode Length _____ Total Episodes _____

EPISODE TRACKER

① ② ③ ④ ⑤ ⑥ ⑦ ⑧ ⑨ ⑩ ⑪ ⑫ ⑬ ⑭ ⑮ ⑯ ⑰ ⑱ ⑲ ⑳ ㉑ ㉒ ㉓ ㉔

Plot/Synopsis _____

_____

_____

Notes _____

_____

_____

_____

_____

_____

_____

_____

_____

_____

MY RATING

New Season Begins_____ ★★★★★

🍿 MY SHOWS 📺

Show Title _____

Network/Streaming Service _____

Start Date _____ Day/Night/Time _____

Season # _____ Total Seasons _____

Episode Length _____ Total Episodes _____

EPISODE TRACKER

① ② ③ ④ ⑤ ⑥ ⑦ ⑧ ⑨ ⑩ ⑪ ⑫ ⑬ ⑭ ⑮ ⑯ ⑰ ⑱ ⑲ ⑳ ㉑ ㉒ ㉓ ㉔

Plot/Synopsis _____

_____

_____

Notes _____

_____

_____

_____

_____

_____

_____

_____

_____

MY RATING
⭐⭐⭐⭐⭐

New Season Begins_____

🍿 MY SHOWS 📺

Show Title _____

Network/Streaming Service _____

Start Date _____ Day/Night/Time _____

Season # _____ Total Seasons _____

Episode Length _____ Total Episodes _____

EPISODE TRACKER

① ② ③ ④ ⑤ ⑥ ⑦ ⑧ ⑨ ⑩ ⑪ ⑫ ⑬ ⑭ ⑮ ⑯ ⑰ ⑱ ⑲ ⑳ ㉑ ㉒ ㉓ ㉔

Plot/Synopsis _____

_____

_____

Notes _____

_____

_____

_____

_____

_____

_____

_____

_____

MY RATING

⭐ ⭐ ⭐ ⭐ ⭐

New Season Begins _____

🍿 MY SHOWS 📺

Show Title _____

Network/Streaming Service _____

Start Date _____ Day/Night/Time _____

Season # _____ Total Seasons _____

Episode Length _____ Total Episodes _____

EPISODE TRACKER

① ② ③ ④ ⑤ ⑥ ⑦ ⑧ ⑨ ⑩ ⑪ ⑫ ⑬ ⑭ ⑮ ⑯ ⑰ ⑱ ⑲ ⑳ ㉑ ㉒ ㉓ ㉔

Plot/Synopsis _____

_____

_____

Notes _____

_____

_____

_____

_____

_____

_____

_____

MY RATING
⭐⭐⭐⭐⭐

New Season Begins_____

🍿 MY SHOWS 📺

Show Title _____

Network/Streaming Service _____

Start Date _____ Day/Night/Time _____

Season # _____ Total Seasons _____

Episode Length _____ Total Episodes _____

EPISODE TRACKER

① ② ③ ④ ⑤ ⑥ ⑦ ⑧ ⑨ ⑩ ⑪ ⑫ ⑬ ⑭ ⑮ ⑯ ⑰ ⑱ ⑲ ⑳ ㉑ ㉒ ㉓ ㉔

Plot/Synopsis _____

_____

_____

Notes _____

_____

_____

_____

_____

_____

_____

_____

_____

MY RATING

New Season Begins _____ ★★★★★

🍿 MY SHOWS 📺

Show Title _____

Network/Streaming Service _____

Start Date _____ Day/Night/Time _____

Season # _____ Total Seasons _____

Episode Length _____ Total Episodes _____

EPISODE TRACKER

① ② ③ ④ ⑤ ⑥ ⑦ ⑧ ⑨ ⑩ ⑪ ⑫ ⑬ ⑭ ⑮ ⑯ ⑰ ⑱ ⑲ ⑳ ㉑ ㉒ ㉓ ㉔

Plot/Synopsis _____

_____

_____

Notes _____

_____

_____

_____

_____

_____

_____

_____

_____

_____

MY RATING
⭐⭐⭐⭐⭐

New Season Begins _____

🍿 MY SHOWS 📺

Show Title _____

Network/Streaming Service _____

Start Date _____ Day/Night/Time _____

Season # _____ Total Seasons _____

Episode Length _____ Total Episodes _____

EPISODE TRACKER

① ② ③ ④ ⑤ ⑥ ⑦ ⑧ ⑨ ⑩ ⑪ ⑫ ⑬ ⑭ ⑮ ⑯ ⑰ ⑱ ⑲ ⑳ ㉑ ㉒ ㉓ ㉔

Plot/Synopsis _____

_____

_____

Notes _____

_____

_____

_____

_____

_____

_____

_____

_____

_____

MY RATING

New Season Begins _____ ⭐⭐⭐⭐⭐

119

🍿 MY SHOWS 📺

Show Title _____

Network/Streaming Service _____

Start Date _____ Day/Night/Time _____

Season # _____ Total Seasons _____

Episode Length _____ Total Episodes _____

EPISODE TRACKER

① ② ③ ④ ⑤ ⑥ ⑦ ⑧ ⑨ ⑩ ⑪ ⑫ ⑬ ⑭ ⑮ ⑯ ⑰ ⑱ ⑲ ⑳ ㉑ ㉒ ㉓ ㉔

Plot/Synopsis _____

_____

_____

Notes _____

_____

_____

_____

_____

_____

_____

_____

MY RATING

New Season Begins_____ ⭐⭐⭐⭐⭐

🍿 MY SHOWS 📺

Show Title _____

Network/Streaming Service _____

Start Date _____ Day/Night/Time _____

Season # _____ Total Seasons _____

Episode Length _____ Total Episodes _____

EPISODE TRACKER

① ② ③ ④ ⑤ ⑥ ⑦ ⑧ ⑨ ⑩ ⑪ ⑫ ⑬ ⑭ ⑮ ⑯ ⑰ ⑱ ⑲ ⑳ ㉑ ㉒ ㉓ ㉔

Plot/Synopsis _____

_____

_____

Notes _____

_____

_____

_____

_____

_____

_____

_____

_____

_____

MY RATING

New Season Begins_____ ⭐⭐⭐⭐⭐

🍿 MY SHOWS 📺

Show Title _____

Network/Streaming Service _____

Start Date _____ Day/Night/Time _____

Season # _____ Total Seasons _____

Episode Length _____ Total Episodes _____

EPISODE TRACKER

① ② ③ ④ ⑤ ⑥ ⑦ ⑧ ⑨ ⑩ ⑪ ⑫ ⑬ ⑭ ⑮ ⑯ ⑰ ⑱ ⑲ ⑳ ㉑ ㉒ ㉓ ㉔

Plot/Synopsis _____

_____

_____

Notes _____

_____

_____

_____

_____

_____

_____

_____

_____

_____

MY RATING
⭐ ⭐ ⭐ ⭐ ⭐

New Season Begins_____

🍿 MY SHOWS 📺

Show Title _____

Network/Streaming Service _____

Start Date _____ Day/Night/Time _____

Season # _____ Total Seasons _____

Episode Length _____ Total Episodes _____

EPISODE TRACKER

① ② ③ ④ ⑤ ⑥ ⑦ ⑧ ⑨ ⑩ ⑪ ⑫ ⑬ ⑭ ⑮ ⑯ ⑰ ⑱ ⑲ ⑳ ㉑ ㉒ ㉓ ㉔

Plot/Synopsis _____

_____

_____

Notes _____

_____

_____

_____

_____

_____

_____

_____

_____

_____

MY RATING

New Season Begins _____ ★ ★ ★ ★ ★

Show Title _____

Network/Streaming Service _____

Start Date _____ Day/Night/Time _____

Season # _____ Total Seasons _____

Episode Length _____ Total Episodes _____

EPISODE TRACKER

① ② ③ ④ ⑤ ⑥ ⑦ ⑧ ⑨ ⑩ ⑪ ⑫ ⑬ ⑭ ⑮ ⑯ ⑰ ⑱ ⑲ ⑳ ㉑ ㉒ ㉓ ㉔

Plot/Synopsis _____

_____

_____

Notes _____

_____

_____

_____

_____

_____

_____

_____

MY RATING

⭐⭐⭐⭐⭐

New Season Begins_____

🍿 MY SHOWS 📺

Show Title _____

Network/Streaming Service _____

Start Date _____ Day/Night/Time _____

Season # _____ Total Seasons _____

Episode Length _____ Total Episodes _____

EPISODE TRACKER

① ② ③ ④ ⑤ ⑥ ⑦ ⑧ ⑨ ⑩ ⑪ ⑫ ⑬ ⑭ ⑮ ⑯ ⑰ ⑱ ⑲ ⑳ ㉑ ㉒ ㉓ ㉔

Plot/Synopsis _____

_____

_____

Notes _____

_____

_____

_____

_____

_____

_____

_____

_____

MY RATING

New Season Begins_____ ⭐⭐⭐⭐⭐

🍿 MY SHOWS 📺

Show Title _____

Network/Streaming Service _____

Start Date _____ Day/Night/Time _____

Season # _____ Total Seasons _____

Episode Length _____ Total Episodes _____

EPISODE TRACKER

① ② ③ ④ ⑤ ⑥ ⑦ ⑧ ⑨ ⑩ ⑪ ⑫ ⑬ ⑭ ⑮ ⑯ ⑰ ⑱ ⑲ ⑳ ㉑ ㉒ ㉓ ㉔

Plot/Synopsis _____

_____

_____

Notes _____

_____

_____

_____

_____

_____

_____

_____

_____

MY RATING
⭐ ⭐ ⭐ ⭐ ⭐

New Season Begins _____

Show Title _____

Network/Streaming Service _____

Start Date _____ Day/Night/Time _____

Season # _____ Total Seasons _____

Episode Length _____ Total Episodes _____

EPISODE TRACKER

① ② ③ ④ ⑤ ⑥ ⑦ ⑧ ⑨ ⑩ ⑪ ⑫ ⑬ ⑭ ⑮ ⑯ ⑰ ⑱ ⑲ ⑳ ㉑ ㉒ ㉓ ㉔

Plot/Synopsis _____

_____

_____

Notes _____

_____

_____

_____

_____

_____

_____

_____

_____

MY RATING

New Season Begins _____ ⭐⭐⭐⭐⭐

🍿 MY SHOWS 📺

Show Title _____

Network/Streaming Service _____

Start Date _____ Day/Night/Time _____

Season # _____ Total Seasons _____

Episode Length _____ Total Episodes _____

EPISODE TRACKER

① ② ③ ④ ⑤ ⑥ ⑦ ⑧ ⑨ ⑩ ⑪ ⑫ ⑬ ⑭ ⑮ ⑯ ⑰ ⑱ ⑲ ⑳ ㉑ ㉒ ㉓ ㉔

Plot/Synopsis _____

_____

_____

Notes _____

_____

_____

_____

_____

_____

_____

_____

_____

MY RATING
⭐⭐⭐⭐⭐

New Season Begins_____

MY SHOWS

Show Title _____

Network/Streaming Service _____

Start Date _____ Day/Night/Time _____

Season # _____ Total Seasons _____

Episode Length _____ Total Episodes _____

EPISODE TRACKER

① ② ③ ④ ⑤ ⑥ ⑦ ⑧ ⑨ ⑩ ⑪ ⑫ ⑬ ⑭ ⑮ ⑯ ⑰ ⑱ ⑲ ⑳ ㉑ ㉒ ㉓ ㉔

Plot/Synopsis _____

_____

_____

Notes _____

_____

_____

_____

_____

_____

_____

_____

_____

MY RATING

New Season Begins_____ ★★★★★

🍿 MY SHOWS 📺

Show Title _____

Network/Streaming Service _____

Start Date _____ Day/Night/Time _____

Season # _____ Total Seasons _____

Episode Length _____ Total Episodes _____

EPISODE TRACKER

① ② ③ ④ ⑤ ⑥ ⑦ ⑧ ⑨ ⑩ ⑪ ⑫ ⑬ ⑭ ⑮ ⑯ ⑰ ⑱ ⑲ ⑳ ㉑ ㉒ ㉓ ㉔

Plot/Synopsis _____

_____

_____

Notes _____

_____

_____

_____

_____

_____

_____

_____

_____

MY RATING
⭐ ⭐ ⭐ ⭐ ⭐

New Season Begins_____

🍿 MY SHOWS 📺

Show Title _____

Network/Streaming Service _____

Start Date _____ Day/Night/Time _____

Season # _____ Total Seasons _____

Episode Length _____ Total Episodes _____

EPISODE TRACKER
① ② ③ ④ ⑤ ⑥ ⑦ ⑧ ⑨ ⑩ ⑪ ⑫ ⑬ ⑭ ⑮ ⑯ ⑰ ⑱ ⑲ ⑳ ㉑ ㉒ ㉓ ㉔

Plot/Synopsis _____

_____

_____

Notes _____

_____

_____

_____

_____

_____

_____

_____

_____

_____

New Season Begins_____

MY RATING
⭐ ⭐ ⭐ ⭐ ⭐

SHOWS I WANT TO CHECK OUT

SHOWS I WANT TO CHECK OUT

SHOWS I WANT TO CHECK OUT

SHOWS I WANT TO CHECK OUT

SHOWS I WANT TO CHECK OUT

SHOWS I WANT TO CHECK OUT

SHOWS I WANT TO CHECK OUT

SHOWS I WANT TO CHECK OUT

SHOWS I WANT TO CHECK OUT

SHOWS I WANT TO CHECK OUT

📶 STREAMING INFO

service name

login/username

password

renewal date   price per month

notes

service name

login/username

password

renewal date   price per month

notes

service name

login/username

password

renewal date   price per month

notes

service name

login/username

password

renewal date   price per month

notes